MISS U.S. OF HEYA

Floating World Comics
400 NW Couch St.
Portland, OR 97209
floatingworldcomics.com

First edition: June 2016
Printed in China.

ISBN 978-1-942801-96-2

Miss U.S. of Heya

by
Menorah Horwitz

Hello!

Are you a fan of fierce?
Do you adore the adorable?
Then there is a woman for you, and her name is the Miss U.S. of Heya!

Back when they didn't have to have ingredients on food packaging, Phyllis Pornschack of Fort Lee, New Jersey inherited a bunch of money from a great aunt, who was like, "do something important-ish with it." Many people told Phyllis to invest, but Phyllis was like, "I'm going to start a beauty pageant. But a good one where whatever I say goes."

And that is how the Miss U.S. of Heya contest was born!! Riveting! The pageant gathers a group of girls and pits them against each other to determine who is the best.

First they have to do something interesting onstage. The pageant handbook defines interesting as not boring, but, like, if you do boring just right, it could become interesting, so it's recommended you don't pay too much attention to the handbook.

Then the contestants have to talk about themselves, because when winners talk about themselves people listen, and if people stop listening to you talk about yourself, then you're not a winner. The whole time they have to wear pretty clothes. This is important.

The hardest challenge, though, is to be completely unforgettable. The unforgettability of the contestant is evaluated by the judges, led by Pornschack, in a very complicated scoring system. This scoring system is so complex that to the untrained viewer it may seem totally random. But it's not.

This book is a testimonial to the women over the years whom have walked the Heya runway. Some were winners, some were losers, some showed up with a bad attitude and stayed in the bathroom smoking cigarettes the entire show.

Study this tome, carry it in your purse or very small backpack. Spray your favorite perfume on it and marvel at how it starts to smell like your favorite perfume. This booklet was meant for YOU.

Sincerely,
The Miss U.S. of Heya committee

Pageant founder and chief judge Phyllis Pornschack on the rules of the game: "Don't make me regret getting out of bed."

The Winners

You should always start with the best and work your way down.

Sharon Safeway will always be remembered for her moving acceptance speech, strung together from fortune cookies. "She proved you could be profound and profoundly lazy," Pornschack remembers, "and that's what this competition is all about."

Regina Roanoke's victory can be attributed to thugism. Prior to the pageant, the judges woke up to find giblets in their bed and CROATOAN written in cranberry sauce on their walls.

Loretta Loughridge was coronated after she sang a ballad she penned about her unrequited feelings for a first cousin. Her ensuing debut album, *If We Go Where No One Knows Us*, went platinum.

Mina Mendlebaum staked a claim on the crown with her borscht belt comedy routine.
Then she got staked.

In her acceptance speech, Bonnibelle Braithwaight thanked her middle school science teacher. "I was twelve, crying as I hesitated with the scalpel in my hand. You told me to dream big and cut my way to the top. And here I am."

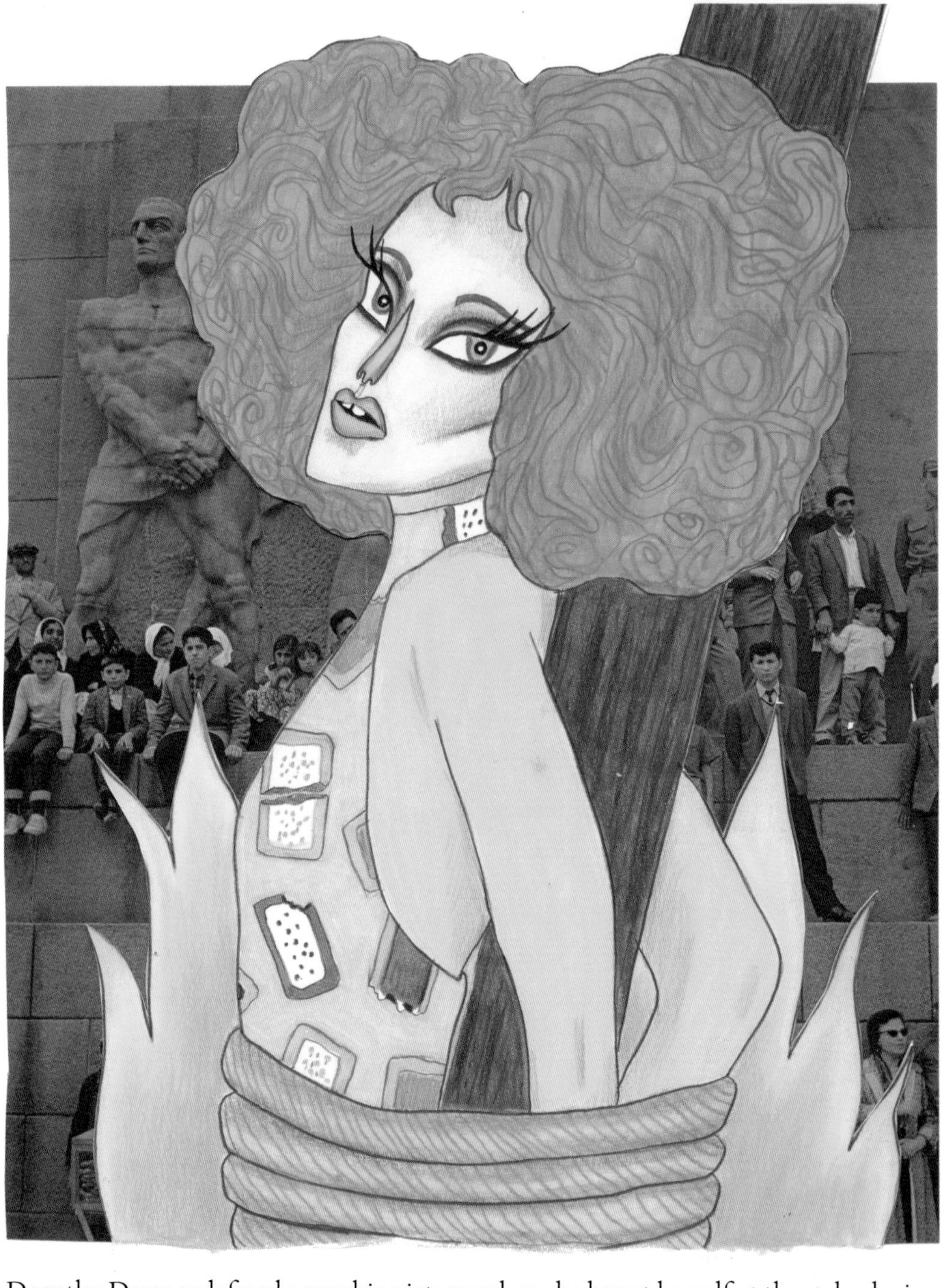

Dorothy Deere redefined a pyrrhic victory when she burnt herself at the stake during her talent entry. “They don’t make girls like Dorothy anymore,” says Pornschack. “That girl left an impression. And a scorch mark on the floor.”

Catherine Cullote declined to answer the panel's questions, instead dwelling on the past while towel drying her hair. Pornschack remembers, "She'd just gotten out of a relationship and entered the competition to distract herself. It was like watching someone fall in slow motion, and when someone falls for you, you fall for them."

The only tie in the pageant's history was awarded to Madelyne Mapplethorpe and Heatherette Haecht. "Some things go great together," recalls Pornschack, "especially two people who absolutely hate each other. You could say the grudge was the real winner that night."

Tammie Temple was not the girl her competitors pegged to win. Then again, they weren't thinking much of anything after Tammie roofied the bottled waters backstage. Karma got Tammie in the end when a stage light hit her head and she got amnesia and then drank the water she forgot she had just roofied.

Esmeralda Ensenada's hypnotic beauty endeared her to the judges, but few realized that she was actually hypnotizing the crowd with her movements. "I studied modern dance in college, plus my parents were very new age. You pick up a few tricks." However you bespell it, this girl is a winner.

Genevieve Gelt, a descendant of foreign royalty, utilized a seemingly simple strategy in her bid for the crown: whenever the other girls spoke, she rifled through her mini backpack really loudly. "I wanted to send them a message. But I was also looking for chapstick. It worked on a few levels."

The Innovators

These girls didn't get a crown, but they probably could make their own out of popsicle sticks.

Brigitte Boule's signature cat eye started the fashion fad no one saw coming, least of all Brigitte herself. "That was a really good year for us," says one animal shelter owner.

Ireland Ingland reached her goal weight and encased herself in amber. She may not have won, but in recognition of her efforts pageant organizers knocked her sideways and turned her into the merchandise table.

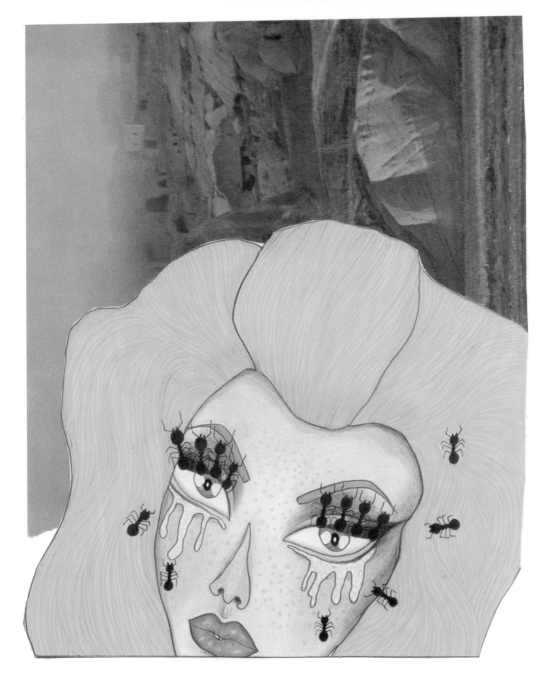

Chelsea Chorizo lost her fake lashes minutes before hitting the runway. In a moment of invention, she dabbed sugar waters on her eye lids, put her head to the floor, and waited for ants to attach themselves.

Tina Teriyaki bombed her interview. Badly. In a bid to save face she said her dad had just died, then began crying. No one applauded her practiced grief harder than her father, who sat in the second row.

Monica Moire had a few helpers in completing her chic couture for the competition. "A pelican here, a seagull there, and a lot of patience," is how she described the creative process. "I tried not to get hit by the same bird twice. I'm superstitious like that."

Gilda Greere credits her unique style to her mother, who also designs all of her outfits. "Mom ate a lot of rubber cement as a child. Needless to say one ends up seeing the world differently. But she's a visionary, really."

The Talent

It's a lot like pornography: you know it when you see it.

Severine Sallop answered her interview questions entirely in menthol smoke signals. She puffed and she puffed and she puffed and she blew the judges away and then threw up on stage.

Jaclyn Josephberg used her time on the pageant stage to complain.

Davora Drudge did a lot of soul searching about what her talent would be, came up with nothing, and decided that if she couldn't be talented she could at least be plaque free. And as she told the judges, "a pop of color brings any neutral palette to life."

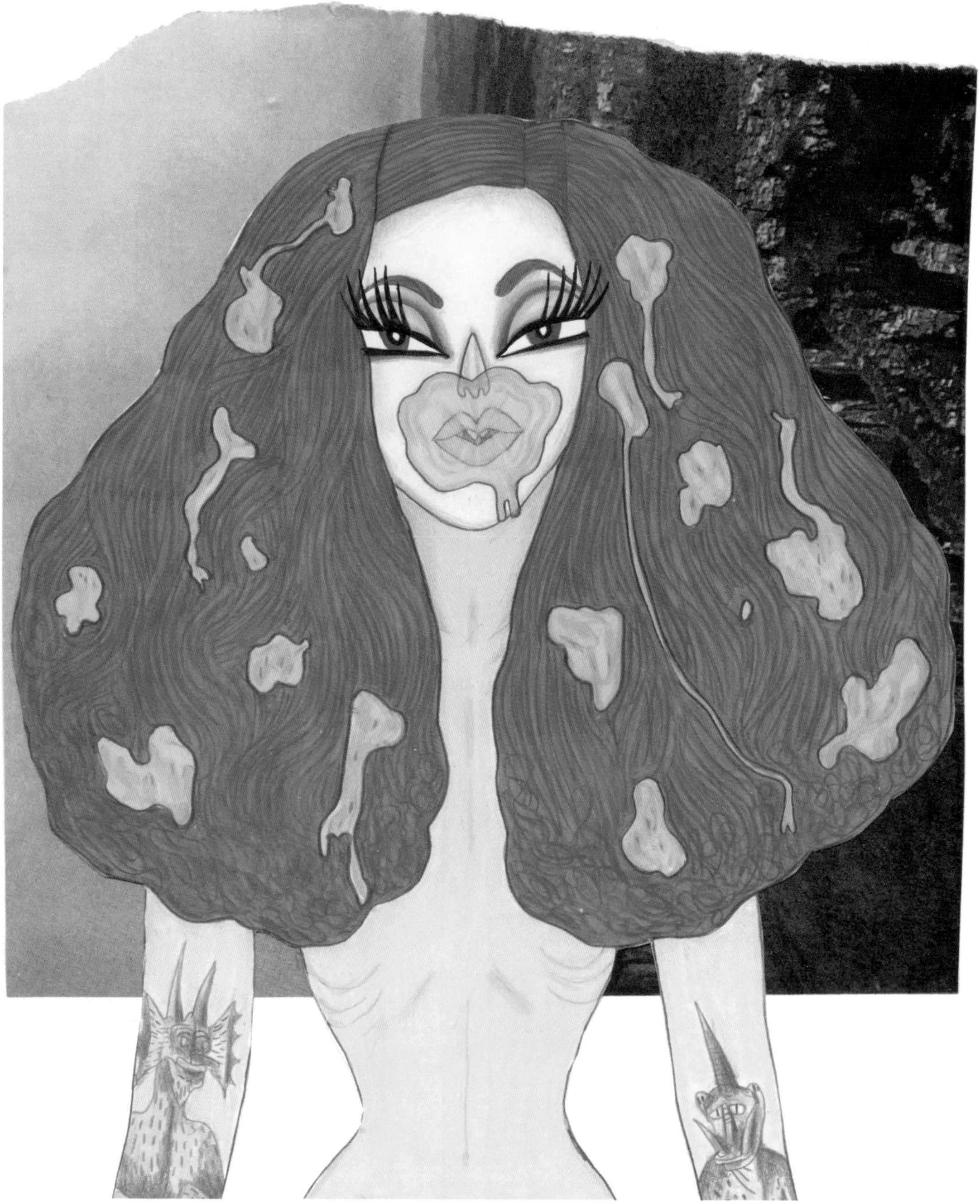

Roxanne Rorschach told the judges that if they squint really hard, the gum in her hair would start to look like a map of the world. "I saw Italy, " Pornschack recalls. "I saw like three Italies and a Norway."

Tulip Tartar agonized in the bathroom before walking the runway. She checked her teeth to make sure nothing was in them. She put on a fresh coat of lipstick. She reapplied deodorant. Satisfied, she walked out, ready to win. "It takes real talent to miss the obvious," beams Pornschack.

Belle Ballachine's talent was illegal to show on the pageant stage. "I'm sure my neighbors are convinced they live in the red light district now. But my real gift is craft. I make these origami birds while he does his thing. The sweat actually shellacks them."

The Losers

The only thing better than winning is saying you should have been a winner.

Jerri Jablonski's lack of commitment during the competition alienated many. Her now famous answer, "I'm not a feminist, but I'm not not a feminist," caused Pornschack to pull out a coloring book from her purse. "I don't put up with a bitch who waffles," said the founder.

Lorelai Leane hoped her sunny disposition would carry her through the competition but she found herself in for a rude awakening. "You're giving me rainbow, but I'm saying 'Reign? No.'," Pornschack told the ingénue. Leane later voluntarily checked into a residential treatment center, from which she has yet to discharge herself.

Nadira Neruda's runway presentation was critiqued as careless by the judges. Nadira snapped back, "I'm dressed to ride a horse, I'm dressed to participate in sadomasochism, and I'm dressed to be in a strawberry picking festival parade. I have things to do with my life and I'm carefully dressed to do them all."

Simplicity Samsonite showed a curated selection of grave rubbing for her talent. "She failed to grasp the concept of pageantry, but it got me thinking," says Pornschack. "We laminated and sold those rubbings as place mats. Not everyone is cut out to be a beauty queen but that doesn't mean that you can't make money off them."

Dawn Dewayne accidentally registered for the pageant, intending to enter the Fiskar Finals, an international leg wrestling competition, held that same weekend. "This competition is about diversity," sighs Pornschack, "and I guess that has to mean lesbians too."

Avril Anaheim's mid-pageant disqualification remains controversial amongst devotees to this day. "Do you know what Venetian check looks like under a spotlight?" bemoans Pornschack. "I could throw a picnic on that dress and the flies wouldn't pick at it because they'd be dead from epilepsy."

Brenda Borgnine's loss almost speaks for itself. But Pornschack would prefer it doesn't. "She could have been a winner. Those death camp hair barrettes? To die for. But she had these ruddy cheeks that made me want to grab a carving knife. Miss U.S. of Heya can be offensive, she just can't be puffy."

The Advice

Apply these queen's words of wisdom to your life. We dare you.

"Take Oceanography. Maybe you're not cut out for Chemistry or Calculus and that's ok. In Oceanography you color in wave formations and learn about dolphins. And you go to the Aquarium." –Rivka Rigoletto

"Treat yourself. Join a cult. Do a drug. Do something that turns off the voices in your head. Remember: if you can't hear your conscience, you can't betray it." –Adelaide Adidas.

"Wear something that represents your mental health. People won't ask how you're doing unless you show them something is wrong." –Ronda Romita

"Formalize your ideal self, then punish anyone who doesn't see you the same way."
—Vicki Vain

"If you can't pick an eyebrow shape, pick them all." –Bunny Brubaker

"Look at the world with rose tinted lenses. It makes everything pink and lessens the stink." –Nilina Neverly

There she goes
Miss U.S. of Heya.
She is stylish
She gives face
She would spray you with mace
Just because she can.
She is walking
Like in slow motion,
Her eyes are deep
As troubled oceans.
She has talent
She has poise
She wears ear plugs
To mute background noise.
It's not creepy to stare,
She's beautiful, she's aware.
She's a winner, she's barely there.
She's Miss U.S. of Heya!!

−The official Miss U.S. of Heya Anthem
Lyrics by Phyllis Pornschack

Merchandise

Available at missusheya.com/store

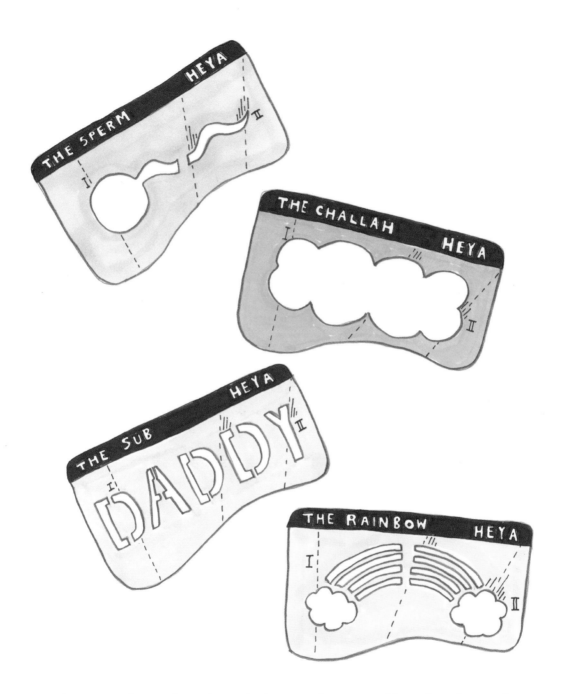

Reframe your face with our limited edition eyebrow stencil kit! These four exclusive shapes will make the world brow down to you! $21.99

Show you're a winner in this Dorothy Deere commemorative T-shirt! Flames glow in the dark! Comes in XXS, XS, and S. $39.99

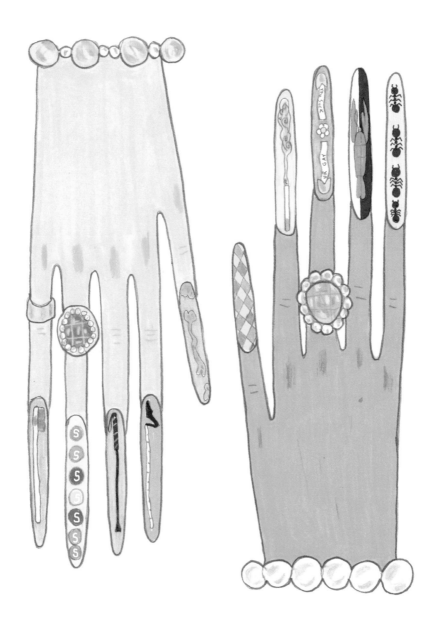

Claw the competition with these nail decals inspired by your favorite contestants!
You gotta hand it to these queens! $29.99

I would super duper like to thank Jason Leivian and Shanna Matuszak for putting up with me when they really shouldn't have.

I want to really really mega thank Seth Hill, Patrick Buckmaster, Dylan Leber, Lala del Maj, and Anya Roberts-Toney for being the best friends I could ask for.

I want to really really thank Davora Lindner, Sutan Amrull, Tammie Brown, Marjorie Liu, Amy Reeder, Robin Ha, Joyce Chin, Laura Martin, Charlie Beckerman, Jeff Poulin, Jen Del Los Reyes, Christina Strain, Elizabeth Breitweiser, Justin Ponsor, Caitlin Moore, and Josh Fialkov.

I would like to thank my family.

Mostly I would like to thank peanut butter, cottage cheese, Rimmel full coverage foundation, Daria, my pillow, my laptop for not dying on me, Lime Crime pink velvet liquid lipstick, and coconut oil.

Menorah Horwitz is an artist and transvestite living in Portland, Oregon. Her past works include "My Boyfriend Walt Whitman," where she made up a boyfriend for a year, and "The Wookie Woof Book," a Tijuana bible starring Chewbacca. She used to work for Marvel. That didn't go well. Her OK Cupid profile could win a Pulitzer. She prays every day for the well being of Shannen Doherty.

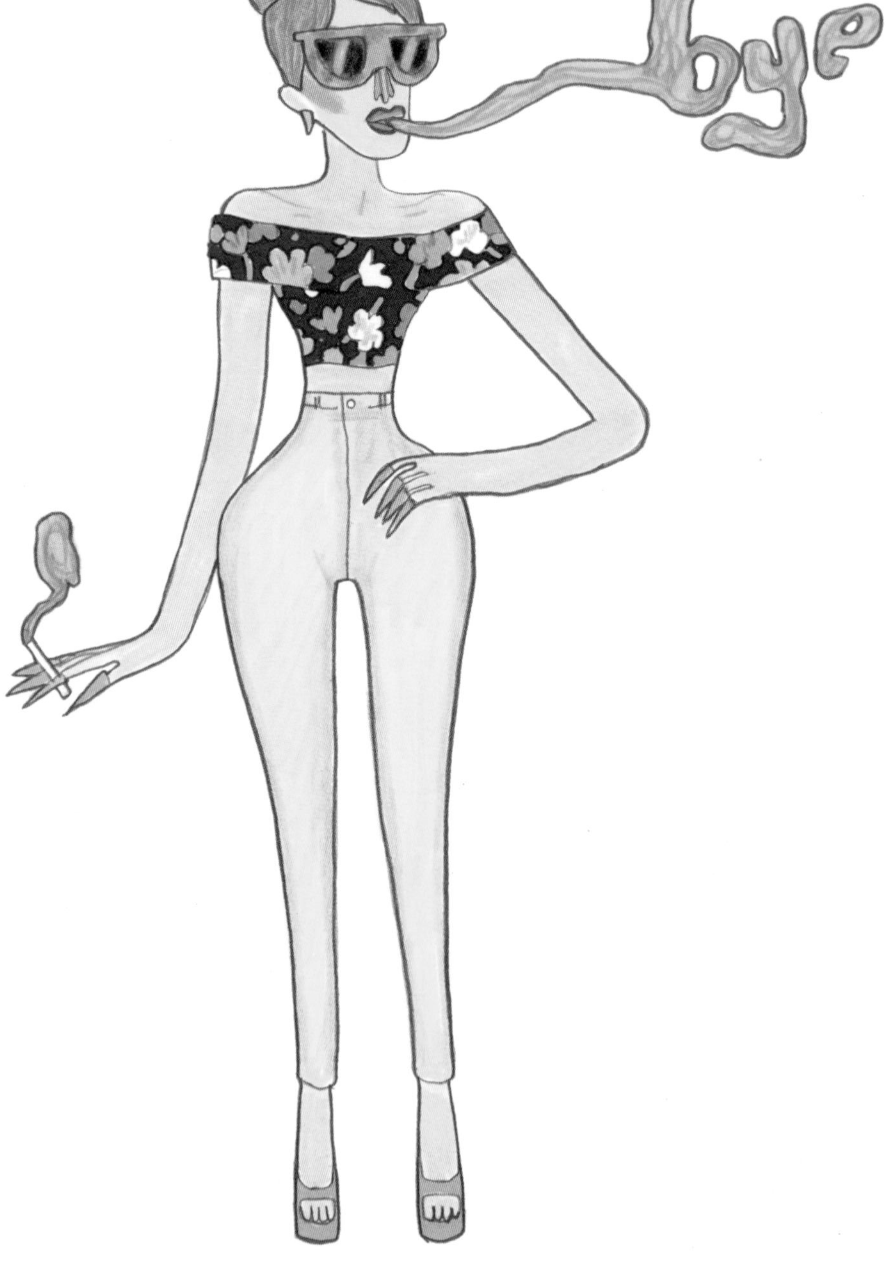
bye